Created and published by Knock Knock
1635-B Electric Avenue
Venice, CA 90291
knockknockstuff.com

Illustrations by Gemma Correll

ISBN: 978-160106818-7
UPC: 825703-50094-3

10 9 8 7 6 5 4 3 2 1

100 Reasons to Panic about Being Awesome

KNOCK KNOCK®
VENICE, CALIFORNIA

1.

sometimes it's hard to be so awesome.*

2.

Dogs and cats always want to lick your face.*

*Animals have a sixth sense about who's awesome.

3.

All your awesomeness could scare off potential suitors.*

4.

somehow,
everything you
touch magically
turns to gold.
Literally.*

*You can always pawn it.

5.

You never get invited to pity parties.*

*You don't have to worry about storage
for a tiny violin.

6.

You have to say no—a lot.*

*When you do get to say yes, it's so refreshing.

7.

Sometimes your amazing attitude bugs grumps.*

*Well, wouldn't you rather be called Pollyanna than Debbie Downer?

8.

Even if you're just placing an order in a restaurant, people stop their conversations to listen to you.*

*Your meal is likely more awesome than whatever they're talking about.

9.

The Dalai Lama won't stop texting you.*

*Takes awesome to know awesome.

10.

So many
good ideas,
so little time.*

*You'll never run out of side projects.

11.

Your charm attracts unwanted attention—at the deli, at the library, wherever.*

*Being awesome has its perks—like a side of coleslaw or forgiven fines.

12.

You can't relate to anxiety, stress, or other regular-folk problems.*

All your exes refer to you as the "one who got away."*

*You're also the topic of some love ballads, a few epic poems, and a novel or two, so that's gotta be an ego boost.

14.

Everyone ALWAYS wants to hang out with you.*

*You're never lonely.

15.

Your voice outshines everyone else's at karaoke.*

*Their eardrums will thank you.

16.

Being a role model is a lot of pressure.*

*But if awesomeness is contagious, maybe someone else can catch it!

17.

The paparazzi won't leave you alone.*

*There's no need to worry about documenting your life if they're doing it for you.

18.

whenever you go out with your friends, they just end up being invisible.*

*They'll get your sloppy seconds.

19.

Your smug parents think they raised a perfect child.*

*They're right!

20.

You always feel so ...at peace.*

*You don't have to waste your time with
meditation, yoga classes, or spiritual retreats.

21.

Your boss always
assumes you'll
deliver anything
she throws
your way.*

*Remaining employed won't be a challenge.

22.

Your thumb is so green that your little garden plot has turned into a rainforest.*

*When life hands you zucchini, make ratatouille.

23.

shopping is difficult because everything looks awesome on you.*

*You'll never have to ask, "Do I look awesome in this?"

24.

what if your awesomeness doesn't last forever?*

You'll have known greatness once—
it's better than never.

25.

Someone might copy your awesome ideas.*

*Imitation is the sincerest form of flattery.

26.

Your social media feeds give everyone else FOMO.*

*You're the bright spot in a sea of bad food photos and banal, misspelled statements.

27.

People secretly want you to fail.*

*Haters gonna hate.

28.

Your awesomeness intimidates others.*

*Better to be feared than to be fearful.

29.

Your awesomeness is a frequent topic of conversation.*

*Any publicity is good publicity.

30.

Being so awesome at so many things makes it hard to commit to one thing. Or two. Or three...*

*You're a Jack—or Jill—of all trades.

31.

Anyone you encounter ends up with a crush on you.*

*You'll never be without a date.

32.

It isn't easy being the most awesome everything—client, coworker, family member, etc.*

*You can let everyone fight for your affection with bribes.

33.

You have nothing to contribute to bitch sessions.*

*You can bitch about that.

34.

Everybody—even strangers—wants your advice.*

*You get to wield the power of a life coach,
advice columnist, and personal shopper.

35.

You make unicorns feel a little inferior.*

36.

Sourpusses want to spoil your happiness.*

*Others can't spoil all the awesomeness in you.

37.

Embarrassingly, you're always picked first for team sports.*

*You also always know that your team will win.

38.

Someone's always trying to compete with you.*

*Life's not a contest.
(But if it is, you're winning.)

39.

once you're on top, where do you go?*

*Sit back, relax, and enjoy the view.

Everybody always wants to know how you do it.*

41.

So many awesome opportunities come your way, you'd need a clone to do 'em all.*

*You're so awesome you'll probably figure out the clone thing.

42.

Everyone thinks you have it so easy.*

*When you've got it, you've got it.

43.

You have so many secret admirers it's a little creepy.*

*You'll never run out of fresh flowers or fancy chocolates.

44.

It's hard being ridiculously smart.*

45.

It's hard being insanely good-looking.*

*Better than being a face only a mother could love.

46.

Your awesome
moves put you at
the center of any
dance floor.*

*Your dance might be a craze that sweeps
the nation.

47.

People constantly worry that they can't meet your awesomely high standards.*

*Set the bar high—even if they miss, at least they'll get closer to awesomeness.

48.

You might get
a big head.*

*Nah, it's just a strong sense of self.

49.

You've never had to go on a vision quest.*

50.

There aren't enough hours in the day to accomplish everything you want.*

*You're so awesome that you can survive on little sleep—and wake up without circles under your eyes.

51.

Your friends silently worry you'll outgrow them.*

*You're graciously keeping your connection to the little people.

52.

The food you cook is so awesome that everyone always wants your recipes.*

*In your spare time, you can write an awesome cookbook.

53.

No one ever wants to leave your awesome parties.*

*You can recruit them to help with cleanup.

54.

Old flames still carry a torch for you.*

*Hello, options!

55.

You don't know what it's like to do something poorly.*

*That's okay. You're not missing anything.

56.

Getting a job is
easy enough that
people assume
you slept your
way to the top.*

*Have they seen your résumé?
It's pretty awesome.

57.

Your awkward stage was not so awkward.*

*You don't have to burn your old yearbooks.

Awesomeness can be exhausting.*

*Even if it requires effort, you make
it seem effortless.

59.

You get so many presents on your birthday, it's kind of embarrassing.*

60.

Your awesomeness makes others feel inadequate.*

*They can see you as motivation.

61.

You're running
out of room for
all those plaques,
trophies, and
other awards.*

*You can share them with the losers!

62.

what if you lose your awesome mojo?*

*You'll have something in common with mortals, if only for a little bit.

63.

You don't sweat the small stuff.*

*You're keeping your dry-cleaning bills down.

children around the world want to be you when they grow up—that's a lot of responsibility.*

*You get to shape the future.

65.

People think you're lying about the good fortune that comes your way.*

66.

unlike the rest of the world, you rarely—if ever—screw up.

*You get the joy of never having a mortifying moment go viral.

67.

Your life is just
so awesomely
full, it's hard to
stop and smell
the roses.*

*Wouldn't you rather be busy than bored?

68.

You can't go grocery shopping without getting mobbed by adoring fans.*

*You can probably talk one of them into doing your grocery shopping for you.

69.

The masses are always clamoring for you to write a book.*

AWESOMESAUCE: MY AUTOBIOGRAPHY

*It'll probably be a bestseller.

70.

Everyone else seems boring by comparison.*

71.

You feel embarrassed by your awesomeness.*

*You'll gain insight into those uncomfortable emotions others feel.

72.

When someone says, "I'm sure you have other plans," they're right.*

*It'll make your attendance that much more awesome.

73.

You're so diplomatic that you constantly get called in to resolve all sorts of situations.*

*You get to live in your own personal political drama.

74.

People are blinded by your unbridled awesomeness.*

*You add sunshine to rainy days.

75.

You're audaciously awesome.*

*Isn't it more exciting than being regular?

76.

People are always wondering what your next awesome move will be.*

*Whatever it is, it'll likely be more awesome than anything they could come up with.

77.

People root for the underdog—and you're not the underdog.*

*Yeah, but the alpha dog commands respect.

78.

Long-lost
relatives will
crawl out of the
woodwork,
trying to sell
your secrets.*

*The only secret you have is how
to be awesome.

79.

It's hard to be humble when you're this awesome.*

*But somehow, against all odds, you manage.

80.

You don't know what a bad hair day is.*

*Think of the money you're saving on styling products, hair coloring, and fancy salons!

81.

Some say adversity builds character.*

*Not if you're already born with it!

82.

when things aren't going someone else's way, you feel guilty about how awesome you have it.*

Even if you try to lose, you win every game you play.*

*Playing with someone so awesome is bound to up everyone's game.

84.

You gotta be you—even if that means standing out in a crowd.*

*If you don't, who else will?

85.

Everyone thinks you're too awesome to be true.*

*Imagine the surprise when they find out it *is* true.

86.

Jealous types watch your every awesome move.*

*You're a trendsetter, why wouldn't they?

Naysayers want something to be wrong in your life.*

*They'll feel bad when they realize you don't harbor ill will.

88.

The Jumbotron operator won't take the camera off you at games.*

89.

You still feel bad about getting the job/part/paramour that your friend wanted.*

*In your heart, you know it wasn't right for them.

90.

You feel out of touch with humanity sometimes.*

91.

You smell so awesome that someone's always trying to sniff the nape of your neck.*

*You can bottle your scent and sell it.

92.

It's hard to describe your life without sounding like you're bragging.*

*People will get a glimpse at how the awesome half lives.

93.

The more awesome you have, the more awesome you have to lose.*

94.

You might lose touch with the common person.*

*You won't have to mingle with riff-raff.

95.

You don't make mistakes, so how do you learn from them?*

*That's just what others tell themselves to feel okay about making mistakes.

96.

Your friends will secretly feel like you're too awesome for them.*

*Name-dropping you gets them
so many perks, though.

97.

You're so comfortable in your own skin it makes others feel a little uncomfortable.*

*C'est l'awesome vie!

98.

AS you age, what will happen to your awesomeness?*

*Like a fine wine, you'll just get more awesome.

A chorus of singing angels accompanies you everywhere you go.*

*They're great for drowning out traffic noises.

100.

Everyone else
wants to be you.*

*They can't! You're you!

Stay awesome.